MARRIAGE FOR THE
LONG HAUL
By Mae Hoover

Marriage for the Long Haul

Published by Mountain Top Books

ISBN 978-0-9962717-2-1

> *Love suffers long
> and is kind; love
> does not envy;
> love does not
> parade itself, is
> not puffed up ...*
> *I Corinthians 13:4*

*H*usbands, love your wives, just as Christ also loved the church and gave himself up for her...

> **So husbands ought to love their own wives as their own bodies; he who loves his wife loves himself. For no one ever hated his own flesh, but nourishes and cherishes it, just as the Lord does the church. For we are members of His body, of His flesh and of His bones. "For this reason a man shall leave his father and mother and be joined to his wife, and the two shall become one flesh."**
> **Ephesians 5:28 - 31**

> **Nevertheless let each one of you in particular so <u>love</u> his own wife as himself, and let the wife see that she <u>respects</u> her husband.**
> **Ephesians 5:33**

Isn't that an interesting Scripture? Men must **LOVE** THEIR wives. But women are commanded to **RESPECT** their husbands.

Shall we rethink our positions?

Other Books by Mae Hoover

My First Cookbook

To Climb a Mountain Audio

To Climb a Mountain Print

The Journey to and from the Mountain

Marriage for the Long Haul - e-book

When Your Mama Calls You Mama

The Fleeced Flock

If I Wrote a Book – workbook

Bad Hair Day Life

Published by Mountain Top Books
A division of Foundation for Publication
Fort Worth, Texas

MARRIAGE FOR THE
LONG HAUL

By Mae Hoover

Introduction

Fifty-seven years of marriage!

What a journey!

Alex Hoover spent 25 years in the trailer business, first as a design engineer for Hobbs Trailers in Fort Worth, later in the international division of Fruehauf Trailers, who bought out Hobbs. Just before

Fruehauf declared bankruptcy they sold the international division to some bankers in Chicago. Alex became the Vice President of FIL working in 17 countries. After that company liquidated Alex went to Trinity Industries in Dallas where he helped design a refrigerated box car.

Some called it the most innovative boxcar in railroad history. That's where the "long haul" came from. We were in

11

the hauling business for many years.

I want to thank my wonderful husband for all the support and help he has given me over the years. My children have kept me in line and given me lots of stories to write about.

My mentor, Patrick Dougher, got me back to writing after many years of silence. My Master Mind group, Toni Allison and Wilma Day, encouraged me.

Many others helped. Of course, I need to thank the Lord for giving me the ability to write and help others.

There are at least three main categories on the path to a happy marriage. In this book we'll explore each one.

1. Spiritual harmony
2. Open communication
3. Laughter

Laugh Often!

TABLE OF CONTENTS

Any book about marriage should begin with the marriage covenant. A covenant is a sacred vow or contract made between two parties. I will quote from a minister's handbook.

> *It is a solemnly unique and treasured moment in life, when two people, who were once strangers to one another, are drawn together by an irresistible attraction, so that their souls care not to be*

henceforth divided by time or space. When a man sees in a woman his dreams of helpmate, comforter, and lover, and when a woman finds in a man the security, companionship and love her heart has been longing for, God has ordained marriage.

Love is the greatest thing in the world, and the rite of marriage is the first and oldest rite in the world. It was instituted by God in the beginning, adorned and beautified by Christ in Cana of Galilee, and commended by Paul to be honorable among men.

It is a sacred and holy estate in which we may not only find happiness and contentment but enter into the deepest mystery of experience and the very Sacrament of Divine love. Those who take the vows of marriage are brought into the closest and most sacred of human relationships. Their lives are blended into one as the waters of confluent streams are mingled, and thenceforth they must share the joys and sorrows of life.

It is the duty of both to cherish a mutual esteem in love, to bear with each other's infirmities and weaknesses, to provide for each other and to pray for and encourage each other in the things of God.

Husband, in your life, your character and conduct lies your bride's happiness. She has given you the most sacred thing under heaven – her life and love. The continuance of these virtues, as husband, which you have shown as lover, will insure her, bless and keep her heart fast knit to yours.

Will you be true and loyal, be patient with her in sickness, comfort her in sorrow, love and

*honor her, in all duty and
tenderness to live with her and
cherish her according to the
ordinance of God in the sacred
bond of marriage?*

*Bride, in your life and love
lie your Groom's health and
inspiration. He will look to you
for cheer, for encouragement
and for confidence. May your
life be the inspiration and your
love the protection he will
need?*

Will you vow that you will be patient in adversity, minister to him in affliction, comfort him in sorrow, love and honor him, according to the ordinance of God in the sacred bond of marriage?

Groom: I take thee, Bride, to be my faithful and loving wife. Throughout the remainder of our life together we will be held in union, loving, honoring, and providing for each other's needs. And I

22

promise to love and care for you until one of us shall lay the other in the arms of God.

Marriage for the Long Haul

SPIRITUAL HARMONY

By spiritual harmony I mean shared religious beliefs, shared understanding of the need for individual meditation and trust in each other.

Marriage between two people of the same religious background, the same cultural heritage, and the same general up-bringing is still difficult. That's not to say unequal marriages can't work, but it is so much harder.

The Bible tells us in 2 Corinthians 6:14 that we are not to be unequally yoked with unbelievers. That picture is of oxen yoked (or harnessed) together which are of unequal size and strength. If someone ties him or herself to someone of a different belief, their wagon of life together certainly won't give a smooth ride.

CULTURAL UNITY

For example in some cultures the family chooses the spouse for their child. In other cultures the wife is expected to live with the mother-in-law until she learns how to wait on her husband the way his mother wants, or until her first child is born.

In some cultures it is perfectly acceptable for the husband to

27

beat or punish his wife if she doesn't do exactly what he tells her to do.

In some religious groups it is permissible for the husband to even kill the disobedient wife or daughter who goes against the required rules.

Religious beliefs are important to know about ahead of the "I do."

When we lived in Mexico a cartoon appeared in the newspaper. It showed a bride riding on a donkey headed for the church and the groom leading the donkey. The second frame showed the couple leaving the church with the groom riding on the donkey and the bride leading the animal. That pretty much says it all.

One young man from Texas became involved with a girl of Cuban descent. I pointed out that the Latin culture is much different than his. He needed to study her culture.

"Oh, no. She was born in the U.S."

At the time his parents lived in another state. He and the girl were in graduate school. The parents were able to come to Texas on a brief vacation and wanted to meet the girl of his dreams.

Their time only allowed them to spend one day with him. He called the girl and invited her to come and meet his parents.

She called her mother for permission. Her mother refused to let her come see his parents.

"You can't meet them on such short notice. They should have made an appointment several days in advance."

Completely different culture, right?

Over the next few months more and more differences developed and the relationship dropped. Had they rushed into matrimony they would have encountered all kinds of problems. Time helped them make the right decision.

Sometimes men can be very persuasive and thoughtful – until

after the wedding. (Of course, that might be in any culture.)

"Rushing" into marriage can be risky.

A number of years ago one of my friends was engaged to be married after a short period of dating.

The groom-to-be claimed to be a private pilot for some well known politicians. He was meeting the bride-to-be's family over dinner a few weeks before the event.

It happened the father of the lady had his own pilot's license and some knowledge of the landing strips in the area.

Every question the father asked about the plane and the strips was evaded or answered in general terms. Knowing a number of pilots the father found it suspicious that the man didn't brag about his passengers, his

plane and other details. That's
what pilots do.

Also knowing someone in
"love" wouldn't listen to warnings,
the father kept quiet.

When the invitations were
ready to go out the man didn't
give any of his relatives' names or
addresses to be invited. The
bride thought that strange, but he
gave some reason that she
thought was plausible. And after
all she was in love.

35

The date was set, the invitations were sent out and the barbecue was ordered.

The night before the wedding the bride was reading the marriage license and found the name of the groom was not the name she knew him by.

Upon questioning, the man finally showed her his driver's license, which had still another

name. She cancelled the
wedding.

She never knew if he had
other wives, or if he was a con-
man. She just knew she
narrowly escaped disaster.

Before marriage the wise
ones study the behavior of their
intended toward his or her family.
If the husband-to-be disrespects
his mother, he will disrespect his
wife. If the wife is belligerent or
hateful toward her father, she will

37

likely behave the same toward her husband. The way the parents of the spouse-to-be treat each other is without a doubt the way your beloved will treat you after marriage.

A certain young man seemed to be becoming seriously involved with a young lady, who fit all the criteria his mother had set for him. However the lady's father treated her mother very disrespectfully. He belittled his wife publicly and spoke harshly to her at all times.

The young man observed their behavior and ended his relationship with the lady. His mother said, "Son, you wouldn't be marrying her father."

"Yes, Mother. I would. I wouldn't be marrying just an individual, but I would become part of another family with all its virtues and faults. I couldn't listen to the disrespect her father shows without it affecting my relationship."

As often is the case in my house, this child was wiser than his mother.

That's probably why "arranged" marriages often work out. The families study each other and the children involved. They seek a partner for their child that will be compatible in every way.

I don't necessarily agree, but I can see the merits of these arrangements.

When "love" chooses, it is often lust or hormones that make the decision without regard for anything else.

No matter how many times you might warn that child that is "in love" they refuse to believe that anything less than bliss lies in their future.

There is another old saying that "you are known by the company you keep." When you are looking for a spouse, look in the places you are likely to find a good candidate.

One of my friends liked to bar hop. She fell "in love" with another bar hopper. They married and she soon found out he was an alcoholic.

They divorced.

Marriage for the Long Haul

She went back to the bars
and found a second husband
with the same result – only a little
worse. He added violence to the
alcohol.

That's not to say that you
couldn't find a loser at church,
but the likelihood is a bit less.

I know one couple that met
over their apartment dumpster,
and their marriage is quite
successful. You wouldn't have

thought such a trashy beginning would last.

You might visit libraries, seminars, coffee shops or business groups for a better chance of finding reliable people.

BEHAVIORAL UNITY

It is a good idea before entering marriage to make a list of all the great things about the intended partner. You could make another list beside that one of all the things you don't like. Then you could balance the sheets.

Are there more bad traits than good? Are the bad

things worth the risk of a
lifetime?

All areas need to be
discussed and examined.

Child discipline is a matter
that should be discussed and
decided before marriage. Who
will be the principal
disciplinarian?

No interference. That is a
MUST! Unless, or course, the

child is in actual danger. A spanking is not a danger.

What church will the child be reared in?

Will the couple tithe their income?

The father is responsible to instill respect for the mother in his children. A woman can't make her children respect her, but the man can. He must do it first by respecting his wife himself. He must set the example. Then he must enforce that in his children.

When our grandchildren were born we lived far away, so only got to visit once or twice a year. We usually stayed only one night or two at the most.

After several of our short visits our son asked, "Why don't you spend more time with us?"

"Because your father would kill one of your kids," I told him.

He was hurt. "What do you mean?"

"He never allowed you to sass me or hit me, and he wouldn't tolerate watching your children treat their mother that way."

"They are very young, and she should correct them at the time if they need it."

"No. That is your responsibility." Afterward he did accept that charge and has done a good job.

On our next visit our grandson threw some food at his mother. Tom took him out into the other room to talk to him about respect.

"Why did you throw the food at your mother?"

Ryan was about three years old. "Well, Dad, I just made a poor choice."

Sometimes it is difficult to remain serious when disciplining your kids. I'm not sure I could have maintained a straight face at that remark.

When Alex and I began dating I was sixteen, and a typical rebellious child. I often sassed my mother and treated her disrespectfully.

51

One time I did that when Alex was at the house. He turned me over his knee and he spanked me – and it HURT!

"I never sassed my mother and I won't allow you to sass your mother."

And I never did … not around Alex anyway.

Whether or not the father accepts it, he is also responsible for the spiritual training of his children. He will be the one to answer to God.

All too often that job falls to the mother because the father neglects it. That does not relieve him of his responsibility.

The Bible tells us a Godly wife can be the salvation of her ungodly husband, but the job is the most difficult and trying task she'll ever attempt.

"For the unbelieving husband is sanctified by the wife, and the unbelieving wife is sanctified by the husband..."
I Corinthians 7: 14

There are many aspects that should be investigated before plunging into marriage. Alex and I dated and wrote letters for almost 3 years before we married. People should know each other and each other's families before. There should be no hurry because you have a lifetime ahead of you.

Before we begin a career, we study for several years – usually four or more years of college. We often do internships or residencies in preparation.

Shouldn't some preparation take place before entering a

lifetime relationship with a
potential spouse?

It isn't God's plan to begin
your preparation by having sex.
That destroys trust and
jeopardizes future happiness.

Child rearing is a big area
where unity is needed.

My husband's and my families
were quite different. My father
was soft-spoken, a man of few
words. Even when he spanked

my brothers or me, I don't remember him raising his voice.

On the other hand Alex's dad, and consequently Alex, reprimanded in a loud harsh voice.

It often upset me when he disciplined our children, but I knew for the children's sake not to interfere. I sure told him later how I felt though.

My mother didn't make truth a priority. We didn't "hurt people's feelings" by being honest. That's how we rationalized telling "fibs."

A friend of mine was told "if you can't say something nice, don't say anything."

A neighbor brought her new baby to show it off. My friend, who was a pre-teen, began cooing before lifting the blanket.

"Oh what a beautiful ..." and she saw the ugliest baby she had ever seen. She finished her statement, "blanket."

If a price was miss-marked on a product at the store, it was the merchant's loss in my mind and the mind of my family.

If we found something it wasn't necessary to try to find the owner. Our good luck and their loss.

On the other hand Alex's family did not tolerate dishonesty even in the slightest. He had a few hard lessons in that regard and those lessons made him scrupulously honest.

His father owned a garage and gas station. He sometimes cut off a strip of heater hose for the whipping his kids deserved. It took very few such incidents to alter behavior permanently.

In the early years of our marriage I remember finding large hams marked less than $1.00. I was thrilled to get such a bargain. Alex took the ham and gave it back to the grocer and alerted him to the other products that were miss-marked.

I learned early in life to be deceptive rather than lie outright. If someone asked me if I did something, I might answer, "Would I do that!"

My indignation <u>indicated</u> a 'no.'

Slowly I learned that honesty really is the best policy. Alex inspired me.

I made so many dumb mistakes in raising the kids.

Tom loved playing with tiny cars and blocks and marbles. When Teri was born and old enough to crawl I told Tom he would have to keep his tiny toys off the floor because if the baby swallowed one, we would have to cut her stomach open and remove it. DUMB DUMB!

We were having a Christmas party at the house and Tom took a piece of that hard candy with the pretty little design in the middle.

He accidentally swallowed it whole.

He panicked and began screaming.

I didn't know what the problem was and so was trying to soothe him when Alex came rushing in and demanded Tom quit yelling or he would whip him. Tom quit yelling, but continued to sob.

Why not? He expected me to have his stomach cut open!
Poor guy.

When the candy dissolved and went on down and Tom realized he wasn't facing an operation every thing was fine.

The next day I went to the pastor. "I can't tolerate Alex having no compassion for the kids."

My wise pastor asked me, "What would Tom have done if Alex had picked him up and crooned 'poor baby'?"

Without much time to think I realized, "It would have scared him to death."

"Then why don't you let Alex
be the man and you be the
compassionate woman?"

Our boys realized Alex was
the way he was and it didn't
change his feelings for them, but
our daughter could not believe
he really loved her because he
used his harsh voice with her.

He believed every child
should be treated the same.

Many years later Teri got two dogs. She called one day crying, "I yelled at my puppies and I never liked it when Daddy yelled at me!"

"Do you think maybe Daddy had a reason to yell at you?"

No sound.

"Do you love your puppies less now than you did before they disobeyed?"

Of course she didn't. It changed her relationship with her father. She now knows love doesn't depend on tone of voice or even disapproval of action.

Tom loved snow cones. To keep from spending more money I told him if he ate more than one it would give him the mumps. DUMB! DUMB!

When he was about 5 or 6 years old he went to a carnival with our neighbor, Timmy, and his family. They were selling snow cones there. Tom had some money and I wasn't there, so he ate three.

The next day he actually swelled up with the mumps.

Now what are the odds of that?

Our son Andy was an accident looking for a place to happen. He had nine brain concussions before he started to school, and we quit counting after that. Today he is a family practice physician, so I guess the hard head stood him in good stead.

One of his frequent accidents was dropping the mustard. He dearly loved mustard. The jar always broke and made a horrible mess.

Alex threatened him, "If you break one more jar of mustard I'm never going to buy any more!" Andy was about 4 years old.

A couple of days later we hired a baby-sitter and went out. While we were gone Andy got the mustard out and dropped it, breaking it, of course.

He began crying. When the sitter found out why he was crying she got really mad at Alex.

When we got home, Alex handed her the money for her work. She jerked the money from his hand, glared at him and left.

A few minutes later she returned with a plastic squeeze bottle of mustard. When Alex answered the door she jammed it into his chest.

"Here. This is for Andy!" She whirled around and left.

We never bought a glass jar of mustard again. And Andy never broke the plastic one.

Just like having kids doesn't come with an instruction book, neither does marriage. Just do everything you can to make your lives compatible.

Marriage requires constant adjustment. We had three children. Alex tells people he has been married to four different women. Each of my pregnancies changed me into a different person. He had to adjust to each one.

One of the worst mistakes some people make is being unfaithful to their mate. One of my friends was able to forgive her husband for being unfaithful after he showed true remorse and promised never to do it again. Although she forgave, she never was able to fully trust him again.

Today there are new ways to be unfaithful. We have the television, movies, the internet and a myriad of books and magazines depicting all manner of mind bending situations. Pornography is a poison that eats away at the mind ... and the unity of the marriage.

Decide ahead of walking down the aisle if time will be spent away from each other.

Will the guy need to go out
with his friends without his wife?

Will the wife continue her
clubs and trips with her friends
away from him?

That's not to say those things
are bad, but an understanding of
what to expect in the marriage
will limit problems.

Will travel be involved in their
careers? Travel brings
temptation in ways that aren't

available at home, or when the spouse is with you.

Being raised in a spiritual and moral environment helps protect the partners when separated.

Consider the career of the spouse-to-be. Does it involve military service? Ministry? With business going global, the likelihood of relocation should be considered. Are you prepared to move frequently? Experience other cultures in foreign

countries?

FINANCIAL UNITY

Alex and I have always
considered money earned as
"our" money. I was a stay-at-
home mom for many years. I
paid the bills and kept the
books. That was more
convenient. It has brought a lot
of stress and frustration over the
years to me.

Many, if not most, arguments in marriages come because of financial stress.

- One spends more than the other.
- No discussion over buying large items before one makes the purchase.
- Not having a budget to follow.

Money and how it is or is not spent is probably the biggest cause of strife.

We have friends that have never joined their money. What she earns is "hers." What he earns is "his." Now that she has retired she has to ask for an allowance. This not an example of unity and now presents an awkward situation.

Others I know hide money from the spouse in secret accounts or hiding places.

CREDIT RESPONSIBILITY

A friend of mine was a collection agent and now owns a credit repair company. I asked permission to use her advice because it was out of my personal knowledge. She has the following wisdom to consider before marriage.

> *"I have many people come to me and say I am in the middle of a divorce or I am divorced and my ex-spouse has put me in a*

financial bind or I didn't know they spent money like this!!!

"Here are a few things you should consider before you say I do;

"Is this person financially stable?

Do you both have the same financial goals, about money, spending it, saving it, working?

"Does this person have a

*diagnosed or undiagnosed
mental condition?*

*"The first thing you should
both do is pull all 3 credit
reports (Experian, Equifax and
Transunion). Sit down and look
at the reports together, look at
their history of spending and
what they are currently doing
about it. Do they have a
judgment against them for past
due child support? Are they
currently paying on it? Do they
have 20 credit cards and are
they all maxed out? or in
collections?*

"Does this person quit jobs
every 2 to 3 months?

"Do they do desperate
things when it comes down to
their finances? Would they
buy clothes before they pay
their rent or mortgage or any
other responsibilities.

"Is this person bipolar,
borderline personality
disorder? Do they blame you
for their spending habits or
when things go wrong?
Sometimes people with mental

disorders have spending issues. When they are depressed they write checks with no money in the bank, check kiting.

"Does this person have their utilities in their children's names? Credit cards in their children's name? Would they put something in your name if they could?

"These are things to consider!! These are the things people come to me with when they are divorcing.

Marriage for the Long Haul

When they look back, they
are thinking why didn't I see
this? Because love is blind
sometimes, but, if you face
these things up front and take
the time to consider the
future, talk to friends, family or
a counselor about all of these
things before you say I do.
Better you know up front than
to know later and you have to
file bankruptcy."
   by Leslie Green
  JoMar Credit Repair
(817)851-5140 Phone

Marriage for the Long Haul

I do have knowledge of
borrowing. When we were
preparing to go to the mission
field I had to go back to college
and earn my degree.

The tuition was very low in
those far away days, but one
semester I did not have enough
money to enroll. I needed $300.
I borrowed it from my mother.

Mother then began to fuss at
me for being away from home

too much; for spending money when she didn't think it was necessary; even for taking classes she didn't want me to take.

During that time I needed a new winter coat, and I made one out of a beautiful cut velvet material. Mother had a fit that I bought that expensive material and it wasn't even "stylish."

My frustration mounted. I
sold the coat for just what I had
invested in the material and
wore my old coat.

Then I prayed, "God, forgive
me for not having the faith to let
you provide for me. I know you
called me to be a missionary
and to be one I need a degree.
So I should have trusted you to
provide. If you will give me the
money to pay Mother back I'll
not borrow again for things you
have called me to do."

On the following Friday Alex came home dancing his cute little soft-shoe. "Guess what?"

"What?" He had me grinning before I heard.

"My boss gave me a $100 per month raise, and it is retroactive for three months." That had never happened before and it never happened again.

He handed me $300 and I hurried to Mother's to pay her back. She didn't want me to do that because she enjoyed the power it gave her over me. I didn't.

> **The rich rules over the poor, and the borrower is servant to the lender.**
> **Proverbs 22:7**

If only I'd learned that lesson and applied it years later. Oh well. Like I have said, 'I'm a slow learner.'

Love ... does not behave rudely, does not seek its own, is not provoked, thinks no evil; does not rejoice in iniquity, but rejoices in the truth ...
        I Corinthians 13:5,6

COMMUNICATION

In the reception line at our wedding an elderly lady gave us the only advice we vividly remember:

"Just don't both of you get mad at the same time."

Alex and I began our marriage less than two months before classes started for Alex's senior year of college. It was too short a time to rent an apartment, so we lived with Alex's parents until time to travel to Kansas.

I had only heard my father use two bad words in my life. Then Mother chewed him up one side and down the other.

Alex's dad used language I had never even heard. I was shocked. He loved to argue with me about politics, religion and anything else he knew would rile me. Then one day I stopped and evaluated the situation.

Yes, he was different from my father. But he had produced my husband, who is one of the finest men I have ever known. Not only that, he had raised four other fine children.

I needed to love him just as he was because of that.

Funny thing. When I quit letting him bother me, he quit bothering me. He quit using the excessive bad language and quit taunting me about politics, etc. I miss having him around since his death.

The first year of our marriage we were the house parents of a men's dormitory at the University of Kansas, and Alex was a senior in the school of Mechanical Engineering. I held a job and he studied.

We had little or no
communication.

When Alex graduated I
was five months pregnant and
grumpy.

When he came home from
work I wanted to know all about
it. He believed he
should leave work at work, so
he refused to share anything
about it with me.

I therefore believed he didn't love me.

I'm not sure when the revelation came that I had to communicate my feelings to him. When he understood how I felt, he began to share things he thought were trivial, but when my only communication all day had been with a baby, it was vital to me.

Communication didn't come easy for us. We attended a

Festival of Faith soon after Alex became a Christian. One of the exercises was to hold hands with your spouse and look directly into their eyes for a sustained period. That was not comfortable.

Just looking one another in the eyes was not fun in the beginning.

Before long we were able to relax and just see the love each had for the other.

After some practice we were able to keep eye contact.

That made communication more meaningful and easier.

We attended a dog training class. The thing that struck me was that you had to get eye contact with the dog. You would point to the dog's eyes and to your own and say, "Focus." When the dog had focused it would usually obey.

I'm not saying 'treat your spouse like a dog,' but we should at least treat them as well as we do the dog!

During our second year of marriage I joined a wives' club through the company Alex worked for. We met once a month and had goodies to eat and then everybody chewed on their husbands.

You know that "when in
Rome" business. When in
Rome you do as the Romans
do. I started doing the same
thing.

We were invited on a fishing
trip with a neighbor and his
family. I don't fish, so I sat on
the dock with the neighbor's
wife, Fern, and did what I had
become used to doing --
Chewing on Alex.

Very tactfully, Fern explained
to me that when she first
married her mother instructed
her not to ever join a group of
women, especially if they were
husband bashers. She said if
you continually bash anyone
you begin to see only the bad
things and soon believe that's all
there is. WOW!

I resigned from the group
immediately. It was years
before I would even attend a

women's group at church or anywhere else.

Even today although I could complain about the jar lids being left off or something else, I turn off my listener when other women begin to bash their husbands.

Just last week I went to a meeting and the woman next to me was what one pastor referred as a "joy sucker."

She spent the entire evening telling me how mad she was at her husband. I tried to change the subject a number of times without success, so I had to just turn off my listener.

At times like that I can almost envy my mother who could actually turn off her hearing aid.

As the years went by, I further learned to meet Alex's needs, as well as my own, through communication. We set date nights, especially after the children were born.

My parents came from a pre-babysitter era (at least in our socio-economic position). Mother felt it was wrong for us to leave the children at all.

We found it vital to our relationship. Often our lives would be so busy we would forget to take time with each other, and I would take his face

between my hands and say, "I
need a date."

In fact I still do that.

He never did take a hint (and
still doesn't).

"Wouldn't a movie be nice?"
I might ask.

"Yes," He might answer,
without a thought of taking me to
one.

Marriage for the Long Haul

It was necessary for me to
say, "I want to go to a movie."

Life got much easier when I
learned to quit hinting and just
say it. At lease I'm trying
to learn that. Unfortunately I'm
a slow learner.

We heard that men who kiss
their wives good bye each day
live longer than men who don't.
If Alex got out the door without
my kiss, I'd run to the door, cup

my hands around my mouth and
shout, "You're gonna die!"

He'd immediately come back
and give me my kiss.

The first several years I was
very selfish. Alex was always
doing things to please me, and I
was always doing things to
please me.

Then one day I was reading
my Bible and it said Jesus came

to serve and we are to be like
Jesus.

I wasn't serving anyone. It
changed my attitude altogether.
I began to find ways to please
Alex. The more I tried to please
him, the more he pleased me.

Only recently a friend told me
that he and his wife write love
letters to each other. They have
a nice bound book and take
turns writing in it. He writes a
love letter and leaves it on her

pillow. Then she writes one and leaves it on his pillow.

We are doing that now, as well. It really is sweet to read how much he loves me after 57 years!

Alex even bought me a love card last November. It was beautiful. For no occasion at all he told me.

He was embarrassed when he read the entire card and

discovered it was a Christmas card.

I still loved it.

We found it vitally important to maintain a love affair, because in a very few years the children were grown, and if people have nothing in common with their spouse, many marriages end.

A lady came to us for advice and told us she no longer loved her husband. Alex asked her to write a list of all the good things she knew about him.

The woman sat for quite a while and could not think of one single good thing. We could name many things about him. The man didn't drink excessively; he was faithful to his wife; he didn't go off and leave his family; he didn't use foul language; he attended church; he had a good job and provided his family with all the necessities.

It is sad when people only see the bad.

> ...Whatever things are true,
> whatever things are noble,
> whatever things are just,
> whatever things are pure,
> whatever things are lovely,
> whatever things are of good
> report, if there is any virtue and
> if there is anything
> praiseworthy – meditate on
> these things.
>   Philippians 4:8

My communication skills are better when I write. Sometimes

I write my feelings. That clears my thinking and often dissolves the problems I was facing before I wrote. Often the letters are never mailed. They have served their purpose. Let's see … who is that communicating with?

One book greatly influenced me -- <u>Lord Change Me</u> by Evelyn Christenson.

The author felt her husband really needed changing.

By the way many of us marry
someone thinking we can
change them. Rarely is
that possible. Only God can
change a person.

As Mrs. Christenson went on
in the book she discovered that
God needed to change her.
Once that happened, either the
things that had bothered her
about her husband changed, or
they no longer bothered her.

I guess that's sort of like when Jesus told his disciples to take the beam out of their own eye before trying to get the speck out of their neighbor's eye. The bad things we recognize in others are often the same faults we have ourselves.

Several years into our marriage, and after two kids, I felt things slipping away. I had busied myself with the kids being sick all the time and just keeping my head above water. I went to a friend to ask for advice.

"I'm afraid Alex doesn't love me anymore."

After listening to me for quite a while she asked, "Why do you think he married you in the first place?"

I thought it over. "Because I laughed at his jokes and I was always positive. I looked on the bright side of everything."

"Is that still true?" she asked.

No. It wasn't.

"Then you need to rediscover the Mae he married."

That was such sound advice. Within days I felt our marriage was back on firm footing. I quit being bogged down and looked up. There was my wonderful, funny, loving husband.

Marriage for the Long Haul

A friend came to me after
reading the verses on marriage.
She had divorced her first
husband without good reason.
She married again and had two
lovely teen-aged daughters.
She was convinced of having
made a mistake by divorcing her
first husband and wondered if
she needed to divorce her
second husband and remarry
the first.

I advised her to consider
her children and understand that

two wrongs wouldn't make a right.

I don't know if the first divorce was a mistake or not, but if it was, forgiveness is a request away. Compounding the mistake by making another, disregarding the children would not please God.

Determination enters a happy marriage. We determined in the beginning we would be married

until death parted us. That
never gave us any other choice.

Now I want you to
understand we have rarely, if
ever, agreed on anything. I
believe it is my duty as a good
wife to submit my will to his.

That doesn't mean I am a
doormat. It means we talk
about decisions. I express my
opinion as to why I think he is
wrong; I listen to his reasoning,

and then I let him make the mistake.

I hate to admit it, but most of the time he has been right.

After we had been married 19 years we became missionaries and had to go through extensive psychological testing.

When done, the psychiatrist, Dr. Charles Fries, declared, "There is no possibility you two can make a marriage work, but since you've been married 19 years I won't stop you from going into mission work."

We have looked at our marriage as a partnership. In areas where Alex excels,

I do not, and vice versa. We complement each other in ministry and in life.

As to changing each other -- I still squeeze the tooth paste in the middle and he still leaves

126

the lid off everything he opens.
When I send him to the store
with a list he still buys 2 or more
of everything, instead of only
one.

My office still looks like a
tornado hit it with piles of paper
all over.

But after fifty-seven years he
is my best friend. I love talking
with him. I love waking up and
spending some "cuddle" time
with him.

He has communicated to me
that I am secure in his love.
Nothing else is as important to a
woman as that.

As important to me as
knowing I am loved is Alex
knowing that I admire and
believe in him. He (and I
believe most men) need to be
appreciated. They work hard to
provide for their families
and they need to know that their
wife understands that.

Sometimes Alex has gotten frustrated and felt like he was a failure, so I took the advise of (I think it was) Zig Ziglar and made a "wall of fame" in his office.

I hung his framed degrees, pictures of his trailers and his boxcar, photos of him dedicating a trailer branch sharing the podium with the mayor of Vera Cruz, photos of each of our children in their caps and gowns at college graduation, and Andy's first medical office. He

has trophies he won: like being
the camp gold brick after he
chose as his jogging partner an
older man, too sick to jog. He
also chose as his "life" verse

> For bodily exercise profiteth
> little …
> I Timothy 4:8 KJV

Purposely leaving out the rest of
the verse:

> But Godliness is profitable
> unto all things, having
> promise of the life that now is
> and the life which is to come."
> KJV

Alex displays a trophy for second place winner in Toastmasters Tall Tale Contest.

He can't feel like a failure when he sees all the accomplishments in front of him.

A woman only feels secure when she knows she is loved. It has nothing to do with money!

Love bears all things, believes all things, hopes all things, endures all things; Love never fails. I Corinthians 13:7,8a

Laughter

I believe one major key to a happy marriage is laughter. Being able to laugh at yourself is important.

Laughter was important even when we were dating. I remember laughing so hard at Alex's jokes or his crazy behavior I couldn't stand up.

Once we were dancing in the middle of a crowded dance floor and he began chanting loudly, "One and two and three and four" over and over.

Of course we drew a lot of attention and I was falling over laughing, as were the rest of the people.

In a restaurant he ordered "fill-it mig-non." Pronounced in English!

We were spending an evening with my older brother and his wife at my house. I was wearing "stretch" pants, which were skin tight. The pant legs worked up. I held up one leg to Alex and said, "Pull my leg down please" (meaning pull my pants leg down).

He pulled my leg and the pants ripped waist band to waist band. It was the longest rip ever heard. My brother gave me his jacket to cover me until I could

135

go to my room and change.
Everyone <u>else</u> was falling down
laughing. Laughing at yourself
is healthy.

When we married I was 18
and he was 21 – almost 22. We
lived with his parents for a
month before classes started
and we moved to the University
of Kansas for Alex's senior year
in Mechanical Engineering.

We became the house
parents of a boy's dormitory. It

was a co-op dorm, so Alex had
to do his share of work like the
other residents.

We were in demand as
chaperones at fraternity parties.

I needed a job to support us
that year. I tried the campus
financial office, but they said
they had nothing. I walked all
over the small town and inquired
at every shop for work. None
was available.

I marched back into the campus office and demanded to speak to the head of personnel. He came out and invited me into his office.

"I need a job and I need it today. If I don't get one my husband will not graduate from the University of Kansas. We will go back to Texas."

"What can you do?" he asked.

"Anything you want me to do."
I always had more confidence
than was warranted.

"Can you take shorthand?"

"Yes." Well, I had studied
shorthand one semester two
years earlier, but I was sure it
would come back to me. It
didn't.

I enrolled in a night class at
the high school in shorthand.

After a couple of lessons I was confident I could take a letter.

The boss called me in and dictated three letters to me. I was really proud of myself.

It was time for lunch though. Alex came by and we went to lunch. When I got back I couldn't read one word of my notes – not even to whom the letters were addressed.

I had to admit my failure to
the boss and he wasn't very
happy. He rolled out a
Dictaphone and from then on he
dictated into it. Then I typed
from the Dictaphone.

I did get enough shorthand
to pass the civil service test,
which was necessary to keep
my job.

The first time I tried to iron
Alex's shirts; they looked so bad
he decided to wear them

wrinkled from then on. And he still would if I didn't take them to the laundry.

   We had to go to a Laundromat to wash clothes. I had an old red flannel gown that was really warm, but it needed washing and I put it at the bottom of the hamper until I got other red things to wash with it. Alex also had a chartreuse shirt. Same thing. Nothing to wash it with.

142

Marriage for the Long Haul

One day he and his friend
Bob had some time off from
class and they decided to do me
a favor and wash clothes for me.

One load had a red flannel
gown in it and the other a
chartreuse shirt.

Every item of clothing we
owned was either pink or yellow
green for many years after that.
I thought Alex looked great in
pink underwear.

In the evenings at the Don
Henry Dormitory, I had nothing
to do except play Bridge in the
main room with whoever was
available.

I worked in the engineering
department of the University,
and they hired college girls part
time to help me.

I worked for six professors.
All the part time girls were older
and had more education than I
did. I had one year of college.

144

They resented me being able to tell them what to do. We did not make friends.

At that time there were few, if any girls in the engineering classes. We lived in a boy's dorm, and except for week-ends when we visited Alex's sister, Norma, I had no female companionship. That was hard.

That was the coldest winter Kansas had experienced in 40 years. It was 27 below zero for

weeks (no chill factor!). I had
never been north of the Red
River, at least not in winter.

I wore everything in my closet
every day, and it took an hour
before my fingers warmed up
enough to type.

We went most week-ends to
visit Norma, Alex's sister, and
Bruce, her husband. She
and her husband were great
card players. Some friends of

theirs usually came over and the six of us played cards.

The other lady would get mad and throw the cards. They argued and hit each other. I had never done anything like that, but "when in Rome…" I took up their habits.

When Norma was really mad at Bruce she wouldn't speak to him – sometimes for days. They would tell the kids "Tell your father to pass the potatoes."

147

"Tell your mother to hand me the salt."

I thought that was pretty cool, so I decided to do the same. The next time I got mad I refused to speak to Alex.

HE DIDN'T EVEN NOTICE!

Of course, I only lasted fifteen minutes before I gave in and blasted him.

Once someone came to the door and asked for Alex during our meal. He got up (leaving his food) and went out. Two hours later he hadn't returned and the food was long cleared away.

Another of his friends came by and we decided to look for Alex. The closest place was the Wagon Wheel, a small bar/café across the street.

There he was with three other guys and a table

completely filled with empty beer bottles.

His friend Bob and I joined them and ordered. Within minutes and before my coke arrived Alex had to go to the bathroom and he never returned.

<u>Leaving me there with 4 men in a bar</u>! And the bill! As soon as I drank my coke (Mother always taught me 'waste not, want not.') I headed home

where I found Alex passed out
on the couch.

He never even knew either of
us was home.

I didn't know how to do
anything in the line of
housekeeping. The only meal I
had cooked before that first year
of marriage was when my
mother went to visit her mother
and I prepared something for my
father.

Marriage for the Long Haul

He ate it, but the next night
he took me out to a restaurant
(which we almost never did!)
and the third night we went after
Mother.

That first year of marriage I
still didn't learn anything about
wife-dom.

Some other things I did learn
– besides how to play Bridge. I
learned how unprepared I was to
be a wife.

152

I was born with platinum blond hair, white eyelashes and white eyebrows. When I was in the 7th grade Mother decided I should begin wearing makeup and rather than draw on eyebrows with a pencil I would have them dyed at the salon.

Because she wanted the dye to last a long time she asked them to do me in black.

Marriage for the Long Haul

People could see my
eyebrows coming down the
street before they saw me.

That winter in Kansas the
color had faded from my brows
and I mentioned it to one of the
guys in the house. His mother
owned a beauty shop in New
York and he had worked for her.

He assured me he could dye
my brows and it would only cost
me the price of the dye. When

154

we went home for Christmas he
brought back the dye.

He set up a chair in the
middle of the living room and all
the guys gathered around to
watch.

Byron put the dye on, but he
made me look like Groucho
Marx.

"No problem," he assured
me. "I can take it off."

Marriage for the Long Haul

He did … along with two or
three layers of my skin.

On the second round the dye
feathered into the raw skin
around my brows and I can't
even describe what that looked
like.

He removed it a second time,
along with a couple of more
layers of skin.

I refused a third dye job. My
face peeled up through my hair

line for months – maybe a year.
That was the last brow dye I
<u>ever</u> had.

When Alex finished school he
took a job in Fort Worth, Texas
(our home). I was 5 months
pregnant.

I would get up and make a
pot of coffee and a bologna
sandwich for Alex's lunch. I'd
go back to bed and sleep
most of the day, or read books
about raising babies.

One morning, still half asleep,
I made the coffee without putting
in any coffee grounds. I was in
tears to think I had failed as a
wife.

Alex assured me it was OK.
"I just pour it out every day
anyway. No one can drink your
coffee."

I cried ... and gave up
making coffee!

Marriage for the Long Haul

My doctor thought I was
gaining weight too fast, so he
told me to drink skim milk.

Those were the days of milk
men who delivered to the door.
Since I was always asleep when
he came he just left the milk on
the step.

I knew the stuff tasted awful,
but I thought skim milk was
supposed to taste awful. It
wasn't until I had drunk the stuff

for 3 months I realized it was sour!

From that day to this I haven't been able to drink milk.

The doctor decided that since constipation was a problem for me I should take a tablespoon of Milk of Magnesia and a tablespoon of mineral oil every night. Talk about bad!

Alex's dad told me he could fix it so I wouldn't even taste it.

All the family turned their backs
to hide their amusement. I
didn't know Kermit's reputation
for "fixing" things so you couldn't
taste it.

Kermit, my father-in-law,
opened a can of peaches. He
poured the syrup into a glass.
He put the mineral oil in and it
formed globules which floated
up and down, like one of those
lava lamps. Finally he added
the Milk of Magnesia and it
clabbered.

I refused to drink it.

"Here, watch me." He chugged the whole glass and smacked his lips. "That was delicious."

Thinking of how terrible those two ingredients tasted alone, I decided to try it his way.

Only he didn't have any more cans of peaches. He used fruit cocktail. That liquid is much different. The inclusion of ingredients was not as dramatic.

The taste was much worse than just taking the stuff alone.

Right after Tom was born I was persuaded to have a Tupperware Party. It was in mid November. I bought over $100 worth of the plastic ware. Alex went up in smoke. That was in 1959!

"Well, just make that my Christmas present," I told him.

He did.

That Christmas morning we were all together at the Hoover's home and everyone asked me what Alex bought me for Christmas.

I burst out in tears. "Nothing!" I sobbed.

"You told me to make the Tupperware your present." He reminded me.

"But I didn't mean it!" I sobbed.

He has since tried to learn to listen to what I mean and not what I say.

I learned you can't hint to a man. If you want something you have to tell him.

I'd say, "Oh isn't that dress pretty. I'd like to have one like that someday."

He never did get that hint.

I'd have to say, "See that dress? Buy it for me please."

Did I repeat that? It needed to be repeated. <u>Men don't take hints!</u>

One year Alex and his dad went Christmas shopping on

December 24th. At that time I was wearing what we called a "merry widow" bra. It was a waist length bra with bone stays.

The two men went into the lingerie department and embarrassed the poor clerk to death trying to describe what they wanted and what size it should be.

Alex spent $40 for a long line bra and a girdle! That was in

1960 and that was a lot of money!

I was mortified when I opened that package. I cried again. (I think I cried a lot those first few years.)

I had a pair of pants that were like spandex (we called them stretch pants). In an effort to make me laugh Alex said, "Just think when you wear that bra and the girdle and those

pants you'll have the fattest
ankles in town."

I did finally have to laugh. He
never bought lingerie again for
Christmas.

Alex had worked in a small
"greasy spoon" (we called it)
when he was in high school.
Late at night he became the
cook, the bottle washer and the
car hop (those were the
days of car hops – but those
days are back again!).

One night a man and his girl friend drove up for service.
They were wearing formal attire.
They ordered a chocolate and a strawberry malt.

Alex carried the tray out to them, but the man rolled his window up a bit and the legs of the tray hit the window and dumped the malts into the man's tuxedoed lap!

If the girl hadn't been
laughing so hard the guy would
probably have beaten
Alex to a pulp. He was that
mad.

Anyway, Alex taught me how
to cook. I got a good cookbook
and began to follow directions.
That was a good thing.

My mother was a meticulous
housekeeper, but a terrible
cook. She had only a few things
that she fixed over and over and

she usually burned something
because she was so busy
wiping up the stove and the
counters from spatters.

We grew up on burned toast.
I thought it was supposed to be
scraped before eating it. Years
later we were at my parent's
house and my dad was making
toast for himself. I smelled it
and ran in to rescue it from the
toaster.

Dad looked at it and said, "It's not done yet. Put it back."

One night I made home made soup. It simmered all day long and it smelled wonderful.

When Alex came home I had the table set and the soup ready.

"Soup!" he said. "I hate soup." He pushed his bowl

back and went out to buy a
hamburger.

    Needless to say, I was mad.
The next day at work
Alex told his boss about my
meal.

    His boss admonished him.
"Tonight you go home and it
doesn't matter what she cooks
you brag on it and eat every
bite. You can't do things like
you did last night and hope to
keep your wife happy."

You know the saying, "If mama ain't happy, ain't nobody happy!"

Alex agreed to take his boss' advice.

That night I slapped a package of cold wieners on a paper plate; opened a can of pork and beans and stuck a spoon in the can. I put a bottle of coke with the opener beside it and threw a package of potato chips on his paper plate.

He ate and said, "Mae, this is the best meal you've ever made."

That really frosted me.

Then he began to act in one of his crazy ways and got me to laughing. You can't stay mad for very long at someone who makes you laugh.

On another night he got mad at me and left the house without saying where he was going.

176

Marriage for the Long Haul

When he didn't come home right
away I made a bed for him on
the couch. I went to bed.

When he came in I had my
back to his side of the bed and
pretended to be asleep.

He had seen the couch, but
decided to sleep in his own bed.

He snuggled up to my back
and whispered, "Hey lady, is
your husband home?"

I got up and slept on the couch.

That was silly I decided, and the next night we both slept in our own bed.

That was the only night we ever slept apart out of anger. Out of snoring maybe, but not anger.

Our backgrounds were very different. My mother was

severely hard of hearing and my father was a quiet, soft spoken man, but a stern disciplinarian.

Our house was always spotlessly clean and extremely quiet. We didn't talk during meals.

Alex's home was full of people and lots of laughter and fun. He never heard the sound of a fork scraping on a plate during a meal until he ate at my house. His family was always talking and carrying on during the meal.

We had to take our shoes off outside before entering my parent's house, so as to keep it clean.

Alex's mother was insulted when I started taking my muddy shoes off before entering her house. She valued the people more than the house. She knew the house would clean up.

Mother was so meticulous
that when I was a smoker and
tipped the second ash the
ashtray sizzled because she
had washed it from the first tip of
ashes.

Part of my rebellion was to be
a messy housekeeper.

When I made my bed at
home Mother always re-made it
because I didn't do it good
enough. So I never tried to do a
bed right (and still don't). I

bought a big comforter. It covers a multitude of sins.

When I have company if the house isn't ready when they arrive it doesn't get ready. I sit down and enjoy my company. The house will still be there when the company is gone.

We had been married probably ten years or more when we had to replace the carpet in our house.

Mother said, "Whatever you do don't buy shag or nylon carpet."

I called the carpet store and asked for nylon shag. That's what I bought. Talk about rebellion!

The night before we married I said to Mother, "I wish you liked Alex."

"Oh, I do," she said.

"You never acted like it."

"If I had you wouldn't be marrying him." She smiled and I had to admit the truth.

Any other person she liked I had immediately dropped. I'm glad she was smarter than me.

Alex is always telling funny stories or doing crazy things even today.

Two of our nieces were majorettes in high school. They were practicing baton twirling in the front yard of Alex's parents' house. Alex watched them for a few minutes.

"I used to do that," he told them. "I marched in front of the band twirling that thing."

"No, you didn't!" They laughed.

He insisted it was true.

He finally convinced them. "Here, let me show you."

He took one of the batons and began running backward and twisting his wrist with the baton. He didn't let it go.

It was obvious he had never been a drum major. Everyone was laughing at his performance.

One of his parents' neighbors had set up hay bales with a

target in front of their garage
and he and Alex's brother,
Danny, were practicing bow and
arrow.

"I used to do that." Alex told
them.

"If you did, show me." The
neighbor handed him the bow
and an arrow.

"The target is too close for
me." Alex walked back about

twenty feet further and aimed for the target.

Miraculously the arrow hit the bull's eye dead center. Even Alex was surprised.

"Do it again," the neighbor demanded.

"No, I don't want to split the first arrow," Alex bragged.

He finally was persuaded to
try again and the second time
he missed the whole garage.

When Tom was in high
school he and his friend Bubba
were shooting at black birds and
missing.

Alex said, "Here give me
your gun and I'll show you how
it's done."

He aimed at a flock of the
birds overhead and shot one. It
fell right between his feet.

"I'm slipping." Alex told
them. "I usually catch it in my
game bag."

He handed the gun back
and declared, "Now that's how
it's done."

On another occasion my
two brothers were trying to chop

down a tree on my brother Joe's land.

Alex watched a while, and then said, "Let me show you how it's done."

He took the axe and attacked the tree. Within a few chops it fell on him – not away from him!

Limbs were all around him and a cloud of dust completely covered him. My brothers stood in shock, thinking he must be injured.

Miraculously when the dust settled, Alex stood there without a scratch. He looked at my brothers. He handed the axe to Joe and said, "Now that's how it's done."

No matter what question you ask Alex he will give you an answer.

The words, "I don't know" are
not a part of his vocabulary.
The answer will be some wild
story. And even after all these
years I still believe him.

His mother was addicted to
the soap operas. She had to go
to the doctor once when we
were visiting her and she asked
Alex to watch the shows and tell
her what happened.

When she returned he had
learned the names and some of

193

the incidents enough to make up
what happened.

He told her one of the
characters was pregnant
with another one's husband's
baby and that one of the
characters had developed
terminal cancer and had only
two days to live, and on and on.

His mother cried at the
terrible disasters Alex described,
so he had to admit he made it all
up.

194

Marriage for the Long Haul

His mother had a parakeet.
His parents were going on
vacation and Alex agreed to
bird-sit for them.

Not two days into the stay the
bird developed a huge tumor on
its breast.

We took it to the vet and he
said he could operate and
remove the tumor for $350, or
he could put it to sleep for $15.

195

"I can buy 35 cents worth of chloroform and put it to sleep myself." Alex declared.

He bought the chloroform and some cotton balls and got ready to do the deed. He saturated a cotton ball and held the bird. He looked at the bird and he looked at the cotton ball.

He put the bird back in the cage.

After several tries he took the
bird to the vet and paid the $15.

Another blunder he and one
of his co-workers made
during those first years of our
marriage was a doozie.

I called the office around
noon and his coworker told me
Alex had just left the
office with his wife. The guy
knew it was me.

I seethed for a while and the guy must have felt guilty and he went in and told Alex he'd better call me.

Alex was playing cards at the time and he doesn't multi-task very well. He dialed me with his mind on the game.

I told him I didn't think his friend was very funny.

About that time Alex trumped his opponent's ace and he laughed.

I hung up.

He finished the game before his boss found out what had happened. Again he came to Alex's rescue and made him call me back and explain.

The boss sent out a memo that no one else could play that

kind of joke on me or any other wife.

One day I parked illegally in town and got a ticket on my wind shield. The ticket was an envelope and I could have put $2.00 in it and mailed it. (That was many years ago!) I put the money in, but didn't have a stamp, so I put it in my purse until I could get to the post office.

I forgot it.

Later I changed purses and left the envelope in the old purse.

Months later I got a phone call in the evening.

Alex had gone to church for a board meeting or something.

The voice said, "This is Police Chief "someone" and I have a warrant for the arrest of Alex Hoover."

Thinking this must be my silly brother trying to fool me, as he often did, I said, "Oh I'm sorry. Alex isn't home. He's out robbing a bank tonight."

"I don't think you understood me. This is the police and I do have a warrant for your husband's arrest."

By that time I realized it wasn't my brother Joe.

Alex had to go to court (not jail thankfully!) and pay $15 instead of the original $2.

Sometimes Alex would come in from work and do a soft-shoe dance into the kitchen. He often wore a hat and he could bend over, hold out his arm and make that hat roll down his arm and land in his hand.

Try not to laugh at that!

Sometimes when I was especially cranky Alex would take on a French accent and murmur, "You little flirt!"

He sounded just like Pepe LePew, the cartoon skunk.

Despite our differences we have always been able to think about the same stories at the same time. One of us will start a sentence and the other will often finish it. Our "joint" stories are usually funnier than mine alone – and I am funny!

Over the years Alex has supported my "hundreds" of business endeavors without complaint. He married an entrepreneur and he is not one.

The beauty of a partnership is mutual support. He doesn't understand my need to keep trying new things and looking for my niche.

He has hope I'll grow up some day, and I have hope he never will.

I often don't understand why he feels the way he does, but we respect each other and give each other space to be ourselves.

We are spiritually as one, although it wasn't always so.

We continue to work at communicating (and it's work!).

We spend time every day laughing. We even sometimes do laughter exercises. We have e-mails that make us laugh and we play them periodically for our own piece of mind. Laughter truly is a great medicine.

So, you might tell me, I made the wrong choice.

What can I do? Remember the list I asked you to make before you married? The list was of all the good things about your spouse-to-be. Get the list out and check it over. Try to recall why you were married to begin with.

Read some good books. I recommend the <u>Seven Languages of Love</u>; <u>Apples of Gold</u>; <u>Lord, Change Me</u>; and there are many others at your local Christian book store. Many churches offer marriage retreats that help spouses understand each other.

Marriage is work. Work on
yourself first. Many times when
you get your own attitude right
the spouse changes theirs. Are
you living up to your marriage
vows? Your first priority in the
work of a marriage is to build a
healthy relationship with your
partner, regardless of
whether or not he or she is living
up to their part.

The Bible tells us to think
about the good things. When

we think about the bad things those things get worse.

For the last six years of my mother's life she lived with us. When she moved in she was a bitter woman. She had lived alone for twenty years, and she had a severe hearing impairment. She went over and over in her mind all the bad things that people had done to her.

When she would begin to tell me the stories I would stop her.

"Mother, that makes me sad. Let's talk about things that make us feel good."

I had six of Norman Vincent Peale's books on positive thinking. She began to read them. When she finished one I gave her another.

At the end of her life she couldn't remember a single bad

thing that ever happened to her. She appreciated everything that anyone did for her.

I'm not naïve enough to believe that all marriages can be saved, but certainly many can be. Again, it takes work.

Ten Cow Wife

A story was told to me as truth by a missionary on a tropical island among many such islands. The girls on his island were exceptionally beautiful. Men from other islands would come there to find a wife.

The custom was to pay the father for the wife in cows. The most beautiful girl had earned her father 3 cows for her hand in marriage. That was the record.

One girl was not as beautiful as the others. She loved to work in the garden and she was quiet. When men would come to find a wife, she often stayed home, not wanting to be embarrassed by not being picked.

Marriage for the Long Haul

One day a man came with a
big boat and lots of cows on it.
She saw him because her
garden was next to the road.
He also saw her, but she went
back to her gardening.

The eligible girls ran to their
homes and combed their hair
and dressed in their best before
returning for the rich man's
inspection.

He looked the girls over, and
then asked to speak to the

215

father of the girl in the garden by the road.

They brought the father to him.

"I want to meet your daughter," he told the father.

"Oh, she's not as beautiful as these other girls," he explained and ducked his head in shame.

"I want to meet her."

So the father brought the girl. She had mud under her fingernails and her hair was flying in all directions. Her dress was covered with dirt from her work.

The rich man turned to the father. "I will give you ten cows for your daughter in marriage."

Everyone gasped in shock. Ten cows!

While they were unloading the cows the girl (we'll call her Ana) hurried home and cleaned up and changed clothes. She packed her few belongings and boarded the boat with the rich man.

The people laughed at the foolishness of that man. He could have had that ugly girl for one cow, or maybe her father would have given her to him along with a cow to take her.

The missionary had known
Ana all her life. He knew her to
be a sweet tempered girl with a
generous spirit. It hurt him to
hear the laughter.

A couple of years passed
with no further word from Ana.
The laughter had never died
down. Then the missionary
decided to find out how Ana was
doing and he went to her island.

The rich man sent someone
to invite the missionary to his

home for dinner. It was a
beautiful home, well cared for,
surrounded by beautiful
gardens.

"My wife will serve food and a
cool drink for us." He directed
the missionary to a chair.

Momentarily a lovely woman
brought in a tray of delicious
food. The missionary was so
disappointed. He thought this
rich man had put Ana away from

him and brought in this beautiful woman as his wife.

Finally he asked the rich man, "Where is Ana?"

"She just served your meal." At the missionary's shock the rich man laughed. "You didn't recognize Ana?"

The missionary stammered. "I don't understand."

"You see I looked at her and saw her great value. She worked hard and I could see how wonderful it would be if she saw her own value. That's why I paid ten cows. I wanted a ten cow wife." He hesitated a moment for the missionary to understand that. "I have a ten cow wife. She knows her own value and because of that her natural beauty has blossomed like the flowers of her garden."

We can all have ten cow spouses if we make them aware of their own value.

As for our marriage:

- Bliss? At times, certainly.

- Contention? Occasionally.

- Laughter? Daily!

- Love? Always!

Remember, Laughter
does good like
medicine should!

**To order more books or schedule Mae
as a speaker:
http://TheLadyInTheHat.com
Or call 817 229 4895**

Marriage for the Long Haul

Mae & Alex Hoover live in Fort
Worth, Texas. Their 3 grown
children and 5 grandchildren live in
nearby communities.

They are both active in speaking
and ministering and enjoying life.

Marriage for The Long Haul by
Mae Hoover chronicles their
57year old marriage. Mae tells it
like it is: the good, the bad and the
ugly.

Published by Mountain Top Books
February 2011

ISBN 978-0-9962717-2-1

www.ingramcontent.com/pod-product-compliance
Lightning Source LLC
Chambersburg PA
CBHW060317050426
42449CB00011B/2520